THE TRADING RULE THAT CAN MAKE YOU RICH*

By

EDWARD D. DOBSON

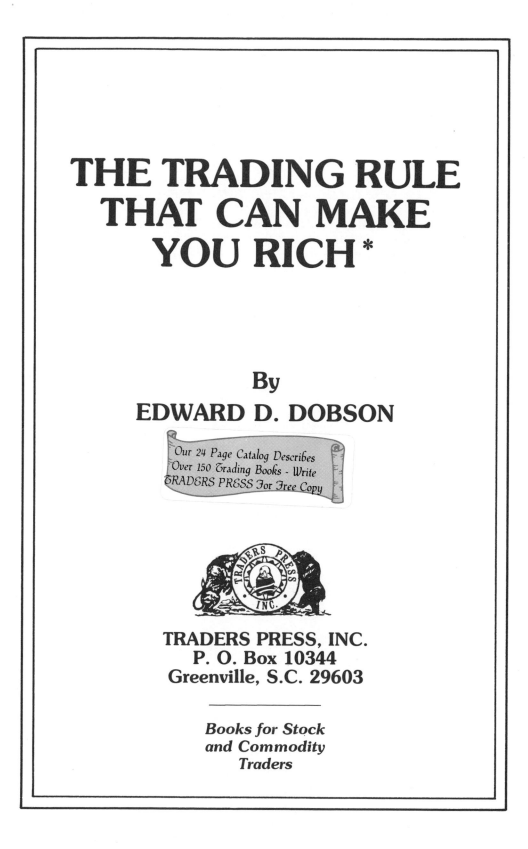

TRADERS PRESS, INC.
P. O. Box 10344
Greenville, S.C. 29603

*Books for Stock
and Commodity
Traders*

ISBN: 0-934380-03-1
Library of Congress Catalog Card No.: 79-64620

Publications of TRADERS PRESS, INC.:

Commodity Spreads: A Historical Chart Perspective (Dobson)
Commodity Spreads: Volume 2 (Dobson)
The Trading Rule That Can Make You Rich * (Dobson)
Viewpoints of A Commodity Trader (Longstreet)
Commodities: A Chart Anthology (Dobson)
Profitable Grain Trading (Ainsworth)
A Complete Guide to Trading Profits (Paris)
Trader's Guide To Technical Analysis (Hardy)
The Professional Commodity Trader (Kroll)
Jesse Livermore: Speculator-King (Sarnoff)
Reminiscences of a Stock Operator (Lefevre)
Understanding Fibonacci Numbers (Dobson)

First Printing, May 1979
Second Printing, September 1985

TRADERS PRESS, INC.
P. O. Box 10344
Greenville, S.C. 29603

Books For Stock
and Commodity
Traders

*This book is dedicated
with admiration and respect to*
Charles Major Ballentine
February 19, 1904 - August 19, 1983

*an old-timer who knew what trading was all about,
and who did more than anyone else I know to teach
me about it.*

WILLIAM D. GANN
1887-1956

*"You can make a fortune by following
this one rule alone."*

TABLE OF CONTENTS

      The trading system described in this
book is, despite its extreme simplicity, the
most effective market entry timing technique
I have encountered during my thirteen years
of experience in the commodity markets. This
is ironic considering the countless hours I
have spent studying many complex trading
methods which employ moving averages, point
and figure charts, oscillators, regression
analysis, and similar data. More ironic still
is the fact that long before I began taking
it seriously in my own trading, I had been
exposed to the primary concept involved many
times, as I am sure you must have. Yet I'm willing to bet that you, like myself at one time, never really took it seriously.

      The title of this book quotes the Master Trader, the late W.D. Gann,
and shows the extreme importance that he placed on the halfway point, or 50%
reaction. To quote Mr. Gann: "You can make a fortune by following this one
rule alone. A careful study and review of past movements in any commodity
will prove to you beyond doubt that this rule works, and that you will make
profits following it."

      My early years of trading were loss-riddled due, in large measure,
to the recurrent error of buying on strength or selling on weakness, when
it looked "safe" to do so, then getting stopped out or plain "scared" into
liquidating the trade on the inevitable reaction, often right at the worst
possible moment, when the position no longer seemed "safe". (Déja vu, you
say?). A careful application of my cardinal timing technique...using the
50% reaction for trade entry, with a protective stop at the 66% level on a
close only basis...should put you, after all these years of searching for
the optimum timing technique, into the enviable position of buying from the
"scared sheep" (or selling to the "scared shorts") at, or close to, the best
possible moment! And, if you don't believe it after reading this book, start
calculating halfway points and watch for yourself ... you'll soon begin to
feel omniscient as you predict the tops and bottoms of reactions within
fractions!

      As always, here's to
profitable trading!

Edward D Dobson

Greenville, South Carolina   Edward D. Dobson
April, 1979

I READ IT, BUT I DIDN'T BELIEVE IT

From the first moment I became interested in commodity trading, which was in 1966, during my junior year in college, I became an avid reader of every piece of literature on commodity trading I could get my hands on. At that time, the amount of literature available was very sparse, and the major work in the field was Gerald Gold's Modern Commodity Futures Trading. I did manage to obtain a musty old copy of W.D. Gann's How To Make Money In Commodities, and in that work, for the first time, read (not learned) that quite often the price reactions that punctuate a trend will approximate 50%. I encountered the same observation in Burton Pugh's writings. Years later, Commodities Magazine made available a brochure entitled "How Young Millionaires Trade Commodities". (Incidentally, I pride myself on being a charter subscriber to this fine publication). Fifty trading rules supposedly common to the successful trader were included therein. And, sure enough, when I came to rule number 41,

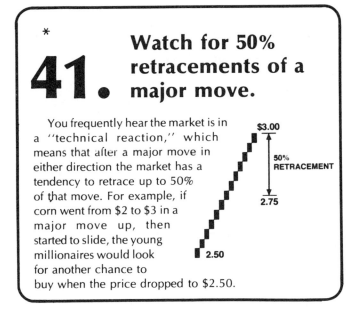

*
41. Watch for 50% retracements of a major move.

You frequently hear the market is in a "technical reaction," which means that after a major move in either direction the market has a tendency to retrace up to 50% of that move. For example, if corn went from $2 to $3 in a major move up, then started to slide, the young millionaires would look for another chance to buy when the price dropped to $2.50.

$3.00

50% RETRACEMENT

2.75

2.50

there was the same idea again: "Watch for 50% retracements of a major move." Each time I came across the mention of this phenomenon, I read it carefully, and tucked it away for future reference.

But, after leaving the drawing board and arriving on the firing line, ready to do battle with the enemy, this idea somehow became relegated to the deepest recesses of my consciousness.

Being technically oriented, the main consideration that constantly stood out in my mind was to "always trade with the trend," and peripheral admonitions, such as "never try to pick tops and bottoms", "...await market confirmation of your expectations before making a commitment", and the like. Thus, having seen July silver enjoy an uninterrupted rise from $2.40 to $3.20 in a steady

* Reprinted from "How Young Millionaires Trade Commodities", a publication of COMMODITIES Magazine, 219 Parkade, Cedar Falls, IA 50613

climb, then change course and react sharply to $2.80, do you think it would have ever entered the mind of yours truly to enter buy orders at $2.80? No way...the trend, which had been up, was now obviously down, as evidenced by the fourty point drop. And, after all, the professed game plan was to discern price trends and get on board. I would have been far more likely to begin establishing short positions on the way from $3.20 to $2.80, then hang on tenaciously as the market began to rally from $2.80, counting on only a temporary rally within the new downtrend. It would never have occurred to me that the 40 point drop just witnessed was the 50% retracement I had read about (but still not learned about!), and that $2.80 was a critical spot to be watched carefully. I would, again and again, be taken by surprise as the trend reversed back in the original direction. As far as actually buying on the reaction, that seemed not only too scary (...look how that market is breaking!) but going counter to the current trend. And, after all, I did remember reading repeatedly how dangerous it was to attempt to pick tops and bottoms.

Now, how could I have read time and time again of such an important phenomenon, and not made use of the information in the "real world" of day to day trading? Well, in retrospect, the answer is not too hard to discern. First of all, when prices are weak, it is human nature to think of selling, not buying (and vice versa)...especially if one already holds a position in the market. Secondly, as important as the 50% retracement is, the sources I have quoted as discussing it or calling it to our attention NEVER PUT IT IN CAPITAL LETTERS, or underlined it, or put it on page number one, or even made a chapter out of it, to my knowledge. Gann, one of the chief proponents of this rule, devotes only a page or so of a 412 page book to the discussion of this concept per se. Commodities Magazine relegates this rule to number 41 down the line, preceded by other gems of wisdom such as #5, "Isolate your trading from your desire for profit," #11, "Try to avoid market orders", and #14 "Don't trade too many commodities at once."

I'll bet that your own experience, dear reader, paralleled my own to this point. I'm sure you must have read in various places of the phenomenon of the 50% retracement. And I'll also bet that you, like myself at this point in my narrative, have not really taken it seriously. I went for ten years after reading about this rule before I _learned_ about it, and actually began entering orders to initiate positions at the 50% level on reactions.

Let me go on record here as saying, unequivocally, that _entering positions on 50% reactions comes closer to the perfect timing system than any other method I have seen in thirteen years of experience_. I almost named this book The PEPS System (_Perfect Entry Point System_), but opted in favor of the title it bears. As we shall see, some reactions stop short of 50%, and some go beyond, and some even develop into complete trend reversals. And this is definitely _not_ a perfect system. But if you can show me one that _is_, I'll eat all two hundred thousand dozen of the May eggs that my clients and I are long at this writing!

What Did It Take To Make Me Listen?

(Enter Charles Major Ballentine)

In the nine year period encompassing my career as a commodity
account executive, initially from 1970 to 1973 with Kipnis Commodities in New York City, and since that time with a major New York
Stock Exchange member firm at my present location, I have had the
privilege of working with a large number of commodity speculators.
Their trading results, as well as their trading philosophies, have
varied widely. Some have been pure technicians, others pure fund-
amentalists. One client who prefers the latter approach refers to
charts as "chicken tracks"! Some are moving average enthusiasts,
some go strictly "seat of the pants", others take interest in a
market only when seeing its prospects written up glowingly in the
commodity section of the Wall Street Journal. (My own observation
of this practice indicates that it is tantamount to arriving at the
Prince's ball just as the party is over and the coach is about to
turn back into a pumpkin.)

One major client, believe it or not, has, for years, main-
tained a second account with a major competitor in order to receive their recommendations. Upon receiving a gem of trading wisdom
from this firm, he will, more often than not, call me and take the
other side of the recommendation. He tells me they are so consistently wrong that it has to be more than chance...they are really
accomplished artists at mistiming!

One thing became apparent over the years...no one system
seemed to work consistently (even the firm referred to above does
seem to enjoy an occasional successful "guess".)

A colleague in my office had a client of long standing who
had been trading successfully for many years, one Charles Major
Ballentine. Occasionally, when my colleague was out to lunch or
out of town, I would have the privilege of servicing Mr. Ballentine's
account, giving him quotes and occasionally entering orders for him.
For a long time, I paid little heed to the trades he was making, as
I kept no set of books on his account and never spoke with him with

any real degree of regularity or continuity. However, I began to notice a pattern in his trading which struck me as unnatural. He was entering buy orders well below the current market level, buying on extreme weakness, and, conversely, selling on extreme strength. Often these orders were entered at price levels I felt had no chance of being achieved during that particular day. I knew Mr. Ballentine was a pure technician in the true sense of the word, preferring never to be "confused by the facts". I had always read that the basic tenet of the technician was to trade in accordance with the prevailing trend. Yet the current trend was patently <u>down</u> whenever Mr. Ballentine was buying, and <u>up</u> whenever he was selling. A closer examination of the orders he was entering disclosed that quite often he would wind up buying right on, or within a fraction of the low, not only for the day, but <u>for the entire move</u>! His sales were timed with equal brilliance.

I began to eagerly anticipate the opportunities when I would have the opportunity of "taking a peek in his hand", and began to ask my colleague to keep me abreast of the positions he was entering. Further observation of Charley Ballentine's trading led me to believe I was watching a genius at work. I had always considered commodity trading a fascinating financial chess game, and, after years of seeing other clients who did their own trading relentlessly checkmated, sooner or later, I realized I was watching a Master Trader at work, someone who <u>knew</u> what he was doing, rather than guessing.

After months of fruitlessly trying to surmise how Charley Ballentine was picking tops and bottoms with such relentless precision, I asked him the inevitable question: "<u>HOW</u> are you doing it?".

And the nonchalant answer: "Oh, I'm just trading the halfway points."

Further discussion divulged that all one need do to pick these levels was to calculate the precise midpoint of the preceding price move. I was stunned. Suddenly it hit me right between the eyes. I had been reading about this technique for years, yet somehow it never occurred to me to actually take it <u>literally</u>.

Naturally, I began to calculate and to anticipate halfway points in my own technical work. At first, I was skeptical, thinking that nothing could be so consistent. But I soon became a staunch believer. A meticulous study of past charts proved beyond a doubt that this principle worked. And, even more convincingly, as I began to anticipate the bottoms of reactions, and the tops of rallies, and saw the market stop, more often than not, within a minor distance of the anticipated level, I knew this principle would always be an integral part of my trading strategy from then on.

At long last, thanks to Charles Major Ballentine, I realized the true significance of what Pugh, Gann, et al had been trying to tell me all along. And what these market sages from many years ago had to say about this most consistent market habit bears repeating again here, for emphasis:

"You can make a fortune by following this one rule alone. A careful study and review of past movements in any commodity will prove to you beyond doubt that this rule works and that you will make profits following it."

W.D. Gann, How To Make Profits In Commodities.

"The 50% reaction is one of the most valuable of market habits and the trader should follow and profit by this most dependable of all market laws. ...This remarkable form of market action is far the safest and surest movement on which the trader can base his moves."

Burton Pugh, Commodity Traders Instruction Book.

It's Been Around For A Long Time

    I have only been fully cognizant of the consistent repetitive nature of the phenomenon of the halfway point for the past two years. Naturally, I couldn't help but wonder if the investigation of price charts ten, twenty, or even fifty years ago might prove this to be a relatively "new" market habit. This led to a close examination of price charts, where available, going back for many years. Luckily, I had much research material readily available in the form of some one thousand life-of-contract bar charts in my own previously published book COMMODITIES: A CHART ANTHOLOGY. The charts in this book cover all of the active markets all the way back to 1960, or to the beginning of trading, if it has commenced since that date.

    Sure enough, there it was, occurring with clocklike precision over fifty years ago (as illustrated by the chart of May 1925 corn). A little reflection reminded me that the period of market activity to which Gann and Pugh had devoted their trading, study, and comments was many years ago, well before the beginning of World War II. Prices were much lower and less volatile in those days, yet the phenomenon still seems as reliable as ever today with the wide swinging, fast-paced commodity markets that we are working with today. And it is working in markets that Gann and Pugh never traded in, i.e., bellies, cattle, gold, lumber, Ginnie Maes.

    The charts below will serve to illustrate the power of the halfway point in years past.

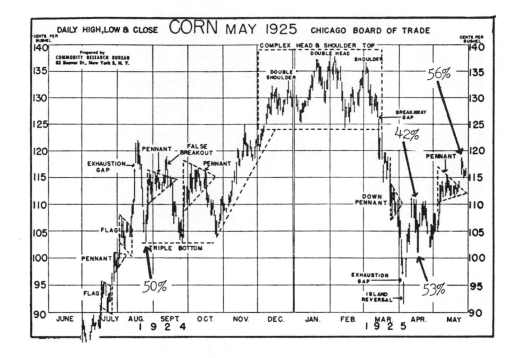

The advance which started at 84 and carried to a high of 122 carried for 38 points. The correction consisted of a 19 point drop (precisely 50%) to 103. This support level proved so valid that a triple bottom set up here prior to the resumption of the upward trend. The peak at 138 led to a sharp drop all the way back to 92. Ordinarily, I would have expected support to develop at $111\frac{1}{2}$ on the way back down (representing 50% of the 84-138 advance), however this did fail to materialize. The rally back to 111 met resistance right where the "support" should have been, and corrected 42% of the 138-92 decline. The subsequent decline to 101 corrected 53% of the 92-111 rally. The final rally high at 118 in May corrected 56% of the 138-92 decline before faltering.

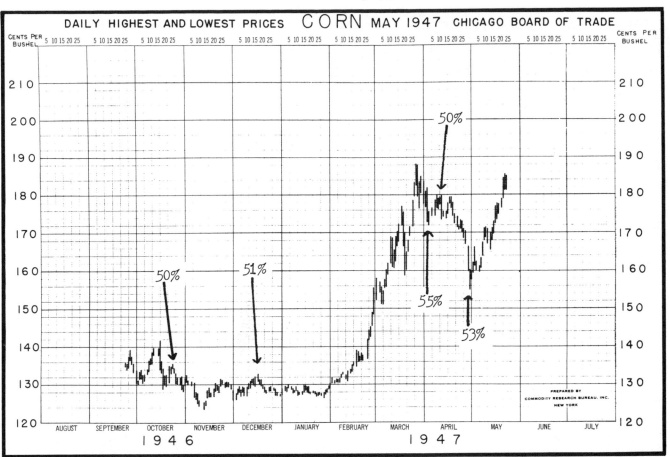

DAILY HIGHEST AND LOWEST PRICES   CORN MAY 1947 CHICAGO BOARD OF TRADE

The October decline from 142 to 129 corrected $6\frac{1}{2}$ points-
50%— to $135\frac{1}{2}$. The October-November move from 142 to $123\frac{1}{2}$
($18\frac{1}{2}$ points) corrected $9\frac{1}{2}$ points - 51% - to the December high
at 133. The January-March move from 126 to 188, 62 points,
corrected 33 points - 53% - to 155. The intramonth move in
March - from 159 to 188 (29 points) corrected 16 points - 55%—
to 172. The ensuing rally from 172 to 180 - 8 points -
corrected precisely 50% of the 16 point drop.

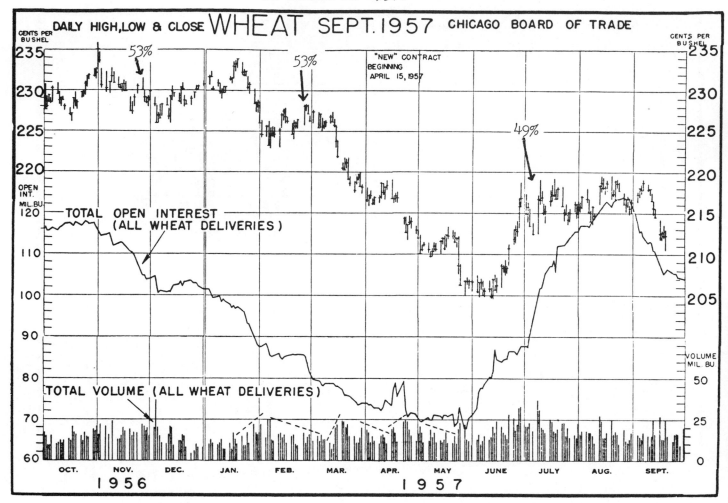

The 236 - 226½ decline in November 1956 corrected 5 points -
53% - to 231½. The January-February decline from 232½ to 223
corrected 5 points - 53% - to 228. The entire decline (233½ - 205)
corrected 14 points - 49% - to 219.

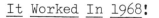

It Worked In 1968!

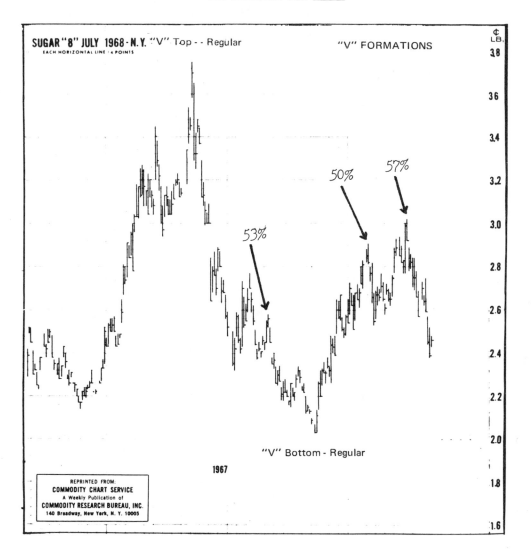

The 375 - 204 decline (171 points) was corrected 57% to
302 (98 points). Note the initial resistance at 290 -
precisely at the halfway point!

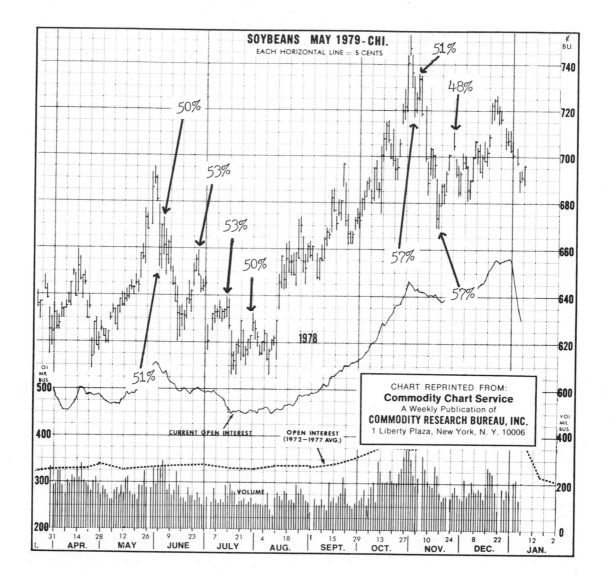

The initial drop of the May-June decline from the high at 695 carried
to 651 (44 points - reached in the third day of the decline), then
corrected 22 points - 50% - to 673. This 44 point decline had corrected
51% of the preceding 86 point advance from the April 22nd low at 609 to
the ensuing high at 695. The entire decline from 695 to 620 was followed
by a rally of 39 points - 53% - to 659. The ensuing decline to 617
(43 points) corrected 23 points (53%) to 640. The July 28th high of 633
corrected 50% of the move from 660 (on June 27th) to 606. The major trend
then turned higher, and clearly moved beyond 50% (650½) of the previous
decline (from 695). The 754-717 drop in early November bounced 19 points
(51%) before continuing to 669, an 85 point (57%) correction of the
entire move from 606. The ensuing rally (669-710) corrected 48% of the
754-669 decline.

14

IT'S AN ART - NOT A SCIENCE

Is The Rule Always A Propos?

There are definitely some markets in which the use of the halfway point has no usefulness whatever. When a market is in a trading range, and during the formation of certain chart configurations, such as a triangle or a rectangle, the rule proves virtually useless. The period during which a market is making a straight line move, without any meaningful reactions presents no opportunity to use the rule profitably, and may even present opportunities to use it <u>unprofitably</u>. December 1971 Corn, during the entire life of the contract, is a case in point. The first five months were choppy and trendless, and the ensuing decline to 135 corrected <u>not</u> 50%, to 148, as would normally be expected, but closer to 150%. Then the decline from 163 met no support whatever at 149, but instead plummeted all the way to 112 in a straight line. Obviously protective stops are in order to protect one's trading capital against this type of situation. A discussion is presented later in the book which shows us where to put protective stops on the positions entered using the 50% principle. This stop level is based on the empirical observation of how far the market will customarily "overshoot" the 50% level within the context of a normal intratrend reaction.

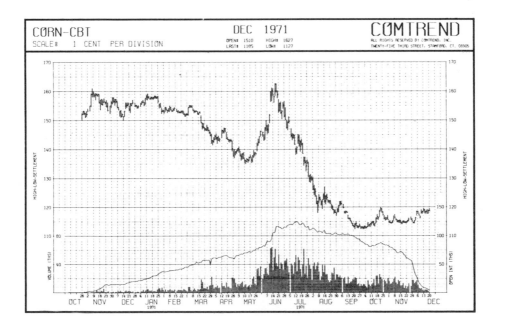

15

What Points Do I Use To Measure From?

There is no hard and fast rule. I try to use the HAP (halfway point) method under the same conditions that I would ordinarily use to filter out desirable trades. First, and foremost, I always trade with the trend. In uptrends, I seek to buy on 50% reactions, and consider only the long side.

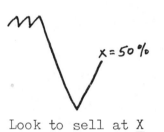

Look to buy at X

but not to sell at Y, 50% back up to the old top from the reaction low.

In downtrends, I seek to sell 50% rallies, and consider only the short side.

Look to sell at X   but not to buy at Y.

The point from which to measure should be a discernible high or low point on the chart. In a "stairstep trend", punctuated by frequent reactions, I usually use the intraday extreme of the last "step" from which to measure.

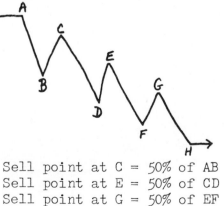

Buy point at C = 50% of AB   Sell point at C = 50% of AB
Buy point at E = 50% of CD   Sell point at E = 50% of CD
Buy point at G = 50% of EF   Sell point at G = 50% of EF

16

I always use the intraday extreme as the point from which to measure, once I have decided which high or low points I am comparing. This seems to work much more consistently than using the closing level.

An observation I have seen work with a great deal of consistency is that the 50% level will be reached, or even "overshot" slightly, on an intraday basis. The closing level of prices will be well above the halfway point, after having dropped down to it during the course of the day's trading, or well above it after having rallied up to it during the day. Thus, you must have your order resting in place well in advance to achieve optimum timing of market entry, or sometimes even to stand a chance of being filled. Many times I have seen a market develop a "vacuum" just ahead of the halfway point, trade down to or within a fraction of it only for a few seconds, then rebound sharply. On more than one occasion I have "shaded" my order to buy at the HAP by one or two points (on beans, for example), had the market trade through my limit, yet receive no fill. A status request produces the "fast market" defense the various exchanges have devised.

Thus, to take advantage of the halfway point, you may wish to give the market a bit of "room", entering your order at, say, 48%. And make sure it's in place well in advance, as there's no time to waste when it's time to act. Charley Ballentine always refers to these orders as "having his basket out" in case "They shake the tree". And, as will be amply illustrated by the charts in this book, "They" often do "shake the tree".

Another market habit that I have noticed with some degree of regularity is that in measuring from minor reaction bottoms or rally tops within an intermediate term trend, if the market goes more than halfway back to the last minor point, the reaction will quite often terminate at the 50% level as measured back to the point prior to the most recent one. This is illustrated by the following diagram, and, using intermediate points instead of minor, by the chart of July 1978 orange juice.

remember

180
170
160
160
160   155 (=50% of 170-140 move)
150
140

17

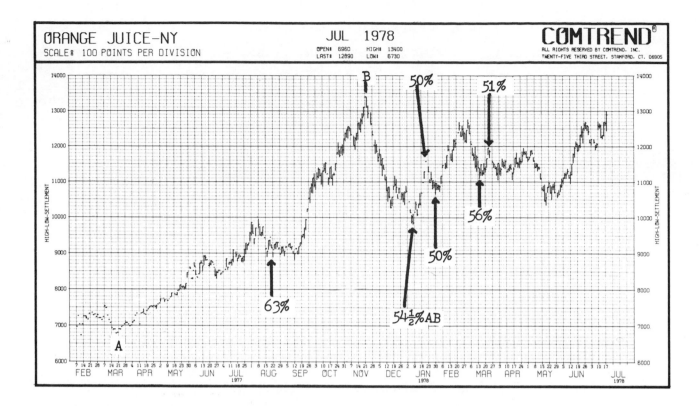

ORANGE JUICE-NY
SCALE: 100 POINTS PER DIVISION

JUL 1978

OPEN: 6960   HIGH: 13400
LAST: 12890   LOW: 6730

COMTREND®
ALL RIGHTS RESERVED BY COMTREND, INC.
TWENTY-FIVE THIRD STREET, STAMFORD, CT. 06905

I would ordinarily have expected the decline from the 134 high
in November to "bounce" from the 111 level (halfway back down to 88,
the most recent major discernible low point). As this level did not
check the decline, as expected, I would then measure back to the next
major measuring point, which was at 68. The decline finally bottomed at
98, which represented a $54\frac{1}{2}$% retracement of the entire move. This phenomenon of the midpoint of the life-of-contract range offering support
or resistance will be noticed if the expected support at other 50%
levels fails to hold. Note that the first rally from 98 carried to
116, precisely 50% back up to the old high at 134. The ensuing decline
was checked at $106\frac{1}{2}$, a 53% retracement of the move from 98 to 116. The
February drop from $127\frac{1}{2}$ to 111 retraced 56% of the 98-$127\frac{1}{2}$ rally. The
early March rally (111-$119\frac{1}{2}$) retraced 51% of the prior reaction. After
that point, the picture turns erratic.

POTATOES (MAINE) MAY 1979-N.Y.
EACH HORIZONTAL LINE = 10 POINTS

CONTRACT COMPLETED BY EXCHANGE ORDER AT 8.14¢ SETTLEMENT

CONTRACT COMPLETED MAR.8	
HIGH 8.59	LOW 5.62

CHART REPRINTED FROM:
Commodity Chart Service
A Weekly Publication of
COMMODITY RESEARCH BUREAU, INC.
1 Liberty Plaza, New York, N. Y. 10006

TOTAL OPEN INTEREST & VOLUME (All Contracts)

OPEN INTEREST (1973–1978 AVG.)

CURRENT OPEN INTEREST

VOLUME

May 1979 potatoes: The 859-735 decline (in April) was followed by
a rally to 794 (48%). The decline to 745 had a one day bounce to 770 (50%).
The bottom at 714 rallied to 763, correcting 61% of the 794-714 decline.
The final rally high at 784 had corrected 48% of the entire decline from
859. The next low (at 708) was followed by a rally to 745 (49%). The low
at 684 led to a rally to 717, correcting the 745-684 drop by 54%. The
next rally (to 734) corrected 50% of the decline from 784. The sharp
rally to 818 went well past the expected 50%. The first decline (last
week of Aug.) stopped at 745, a 51% correction of the advance from 675.
The October rally from 575-677 corrected 42% of the drop from 818. The
617 low in December corrected 54% of the 562-682 advance. The December
high of 687 retraced 49% of the 818-562 drop. The January high at 735
retraced 58% of the life-of-contract range. The 654 low corrected the
whole rally by 47%. The 687 low (week of Feb. 16) corrected the previous
advance by 48%. The 702 low (March 2) corrected the previous advance by
49%.

19

Averaging Multiple Measuring Points

A problem you will sometimes encounter is selecting the most relevant point from which to measure, if there are several available from which to choose. This is especially so if the most recent measuring point is close to a recent top, for example, and the market looks as if it is "ripe" for an appreciable reaction rather than a shallow one. A technique I often find appropriate in this circumstance is to take the 50% level of several available measuring points, then <u>average</u> them to get a "midrange" level of various possible halfway points at which the reaction might be deemed likely to get support. Often this will give you a close approximation of the final support level which does prove successful in reversing the decline.

. 50% CD ⎫ AVERAGE
. 50% BD ⎬ THESE
. 50% AD ⎭ THREE

Equilibrium Is A Rare Occurrence

If one extends the 50% principle to each succeeding move, this would obviously lead in short order to a state of euiliibrium and complete absence of price movement.

As the resulting triangular configuration is an occasional manifestation of market action but never lasts for long or recurs with any great degree of regularity in any given market, we must take care not to be so taken with the reliability of the halfway point as to expect it to work every time the market changes course. Part of the "art" of applying this principle effectively is in "sensing" when its use is appropriate in predicting tops and bottoms, and in learning to filter out situations where it is not appropriate. This, I can't begin to set down on paper...experience and "seat of the pants" trading savvy are necessary prerequisites to learning this art.

PEPS: The Precise Entry Point System

As stated before, there is no trading system, no matter how complex or how well thought out, that always works. Some are much more efficient than others. In my opinion my system, described here, is one of the finest market entry systems to be found, despite its self professed shortcomings. Nevertheless, even the best trading systems are sometimes "all wet". And when the system we are following doesn't do its job, we must adhere to a strictly disciplined system for limiting losses. Preservation of your trading capital is of paramount importance, and, in my opinion, should take precedence over the pursuit of profits as the number one trading objective. My opinion is well substantiated, having seen many traders who didn't think so "wiped out". They were so preoccupied with the "reward" side of the coin that they consistently forgot there was a "risk" side.

OK, here goes, here's my system: (Which I hereby dub the PEPS system):

We will (normally) be concerned with the most recent price move, as measured from the last low or high of consequence. Once the measuring points have been chosen (admittedly a subjective, highly ambiguous task in some instances), it is a simple matter.

(1). Determine the length (LOM) of the price move we are using. This is determined in uptrends by subtracting the low measuring point (LMP- beginning point of the move) from the high measuring point (HMP - high attained by the move). In downtrends, the same procedure would be followed, except that the HMP would represent the beginning point of the move, and the LMP would represent the lowest point attained. This cannot be quantified in either case until we can discern, purely by observation, that a high point or low point for the current move has been reached. We would be alert to the possibility that this is the case as soon as a reaction sets in.

(2). As soon as the end (albeit temporary) of the current move is discernible and the length (LOM) thereof ascertained, we multiply LOM by the percentages listed below to determine our market entry points.

(a) If a small trader, dealing in only one contract of each commodity, enter at the 50% level. This level is determined by subtracting 50% of LOM from the HMP if buying, and by adding 50% of the LOM to the LMP if selling. If the dollar risk is deemed tolerable, and the trend appears well defined, enter at the 45% level. The dollar risk may be determined by ascertaining the distance to the stop point as discussed in point (3) below.

(b) If the position you contemplate establishing is divisible by 2 (2 contracts, 6 contracts, etc.), enter one half ($\frac{1}{2}$) of the intended position at the 45% level, and the second half at the 55% level, if reached.

(c) If your intended position is divisible by 3 (3,6,9,12 etc) enter in 3 phases, at the 45%, 50%, and 55% levels.

(d) Obviously the above strategies may lead to the establishment of only a portion of your intended position, or, because of the arbitrarily chosen points, to missing it altogether. However, a careful examination of the charts throughout this book will reveal that these points will put you into the market at, or near, the optimum level in a significant number of cases. And consider the timing strategy this is forcing you to take. Instead of buying when it appears "safe", and the market is moving in the intended direction, only to be caught by and your equity impaired by the ensuing reaction, we are entering very near the bottom (or top) of a reaction within the prevailing price trend. In essence, we are keeping our powder dry until the most appropriate possible time for entering the market, as observed empirically by noting that a majority of price reactions terminate in the 45%-55% range.

(3). Now, it is intuitively apparent that some reactions which at first appear to be normal reactions approxmiating 40% to 60% will turn out to be true trend reversals and will keep right on going, establishing a new trend direction. I have arbitrarily chosen the 66% level, on a close-only basis, as the point at which to "abandon ship" on positions entered using the PEPS system. Some "normal" reactions do go beyond this point, and reverse back to the original direction,

but <u>by</u> <u>far</u> <u>the</u> <u>majority</u> <u>stop</u> <u>before</u> <u>reaching</u> <u>66%</u>, especially on a
closing basis. Again, this may be determined by examination of the
charts throughout this book, and by any other charts you care to
examine. You may choose to use a <u>straight</u> <u>stop</u> at the 66% level, or
even to give the market slightly more "room" (e.g., to 71%). As you
observe and work with this system in the future, use the stop level
that you feel most comfortable with and most confident of...but be
absolutely sure that you <u>always</u> <u>use</u> <u>a</u> <u>stop</u> <u>to</u> <u>protect</u> <u>your</u> <u>capital</u>.
<u>Not</u> doing so is one of the worst mistakes a trader can make. Aside
from the fact that no trade should ever be entered without the use
of a protective stop, it should be realized that this system's
success is predicated on picking within a fine tolerance level the
end of a short term price trend. <u>And</u> <u>all</u> <u>long</u> <u>term</u> <u>price</u> <u>trends</u> <u>start</u>
<u>out</u> <u>as</u> <u>short</u> <u>term</u> <u>trends</u> <u>that</u> <u>keep</u> <u>going</u>.

Based on our <u>average</u> entry point of 50%, this stop level confines
our risk factor to a very modest amount which <u>approximates</u> <u>16%</u> of the
length of the preceding move.

If bellies have moved up seven cents then begin to react, we
are attempting to enter the market near the bottom of the reaction,
with an approximate risk of only <u>112</u> <u>points</u> (700 points x 16%=112).

If beans have dropped $24\frac{1}{2}$ points, then rally (within a downtrend),
we attempt to sell at the top of the ensuing rally (<u>near</u> the top, I
should say) with a risk approximating 4 points ($24\frac{1}{2}$ x 16% = 3.92).

Another example: Oil has risen 344 points without a reaction,
from 20.00 to 23.44. Finally the reaction comes. Our average calculated
entry point would be at 21.72 (344 x 50% = 172) with a close-only stop
at 21.17 (344 x 16% = 55...21.72-.55 = 21.17).

23.44

Buy at 50% = 21.72
Stop at 21.17 (close only)

20.00

THE WORLD'S SIMPLEST TRADING SYSTEM? (Short of throwing darts)

I'm sure that many of you keep a busy schedule, and unless you have a special affinity for the realm of higher mathmatics, would prefer to utilize an M.O. (that's "Joe Friday" for method of operation) in your trading plan that is as straightforward, simple, and as easily understood as possible. Although I am personally inclined to base my trading decisions primarily on purely technical criteria, I find myself totally unamused at the prospect of having to wade through complex, arduous daily computations of such devices as exponentially weighted moving averages, regression analysis, velocity-acceleration oscillators and chi-square tests!

Consider the simplicity of my method, the PEPS system. It basically consists of trading with the prevailing trend, and entering the market only on reactions approximating 50% from the last high or low point. Protective stops should be placed at the 66% level, as discussed elsewhere in the text. The method is simplicity itself. However, for the novice practitioner, the ensuing illustrations should prove useful.

Our first step is to select our measuring points, which will normally be the beginning of the most recent move, and the high or low attained on the move. Next, determine the length of the move (LOM), which is simply the difference between the measuring points. Then, multiply the LOM by the desired percentage. In uptrends, subtract %LOM from the high measuring point (HMP). In downtrends, add %LOM to the low measuring point (LMP).

Assume an uptrending wheat market, with an initial advance out of consolidation from a low point of $422\frac{1}{2}$ (LMP), to a subsequent high of 456 3/4 (HMP). Thus the initial move (LOM) is $34\frac{1}{4}$ points. To establish different percentage levels during the reaction which follows, we would multiply $34\frac{1}{4}$ by the desired percentage, and subtract from 456 3/4 (HMP). Thus, 50% of $34\frac{1}{4}$ is 17 1/8, and the halfway point would be 439 5/8 (456 3/4 - 17 1/8). This would be our expected support level, give or take a point or two. A good spot for a buy order might be $440\frac{1}{2}$, just ahead of the halfway point. The stop I recommend at the 66% level would be placed at 434 1/8 ($456\ 3/4 - 66\% \times 34\frac{1}{4} = 434\ 1/8$) on a close only basis. Using the 45%/55% method discussed earlier in the text would give buy points at $441\frac{1}{2}$ ($456\ 3/4 - 15.41$) and at 438 ($456\ 3/4 - 18.84$). Assume a reaction low of 437 and a subsequent secondary high of $473\frac{1}{2}$ whereupon another reaction sets in. We now begin looking for a fresh market entry point. We would establish our buying and stop levels in the following manner: The move measures $36\frac{1}{2}$ points ($473\frac{1}{2} - 437$).

$45\% \times 36\frac{1}{2} = 16.43$	$473\frac{1}{2} - 16.43 = 457$	Buy
$50\% \times 36\frac{1}{2} = 18.25$	$473\frac{1}{2} - 18.25 = 455\frac{1}{4}$	Buy
$55\% \times 36\frac{1}{2} = 20.08$	$473\frac{1}{2} - 20.08 = 453\frac{1}{2}$	Buy
$66\% \times 36\frac{1}{2} = 24.09$	$473\frac{1}{2} - 24.09 = 449\frac{1}{2}$	Sell (close only)

Assume a downtrending lumber market, with an initial decline from a peak of 234.2 to a low of 221.8. If we are convinced the trend has turned down, we might well expect the first rally to halt around the 228.0 level, figured as follows: The decline measures 12.4 points (234.2 - 221.8). A 50% rally would carry for 6.2 points. 221.8 + 6.2 = 228.0 Our 45%/55% method would yield sell points at 227.4 (221.8 + 5.58) and at 228.6 (221.8 + 6.82). Our 66% stop would be placed at 230.0 (close only) (221.8 + 8.18). If we assume a 228 rally peak and a second downleg which terminates at 211.5 followed by a rally, we look for new short

entry points as follows: The move was 16.5 points (228.0 -211.5 = 16.5).
The 45%, 50%, 55%, and 66% levels would be calculated as follows:

16.5 x 45% = 7.42 + 211.5 = 218.9 Sell
16.5 x 50% = 8.25 + 211.5 = 219.8 Sell
16.5 x 55% = 9.08 + 211.5 = 220.6 Sell
16.5 x 66% = 10.89+ 211.5 = 222.4 Buy (close only)

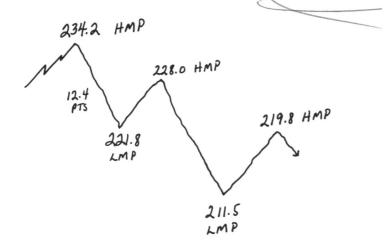

234.2 HMP
12.4 PTS
228.0 HMP
221.8 LMP
219.8 HMP
211.5 LMP

Does anyone recognize
a close resemblance to
May 1979 lumber here?

Now ... if this system taxes you too much, and you find it
too involved, I suggest you delegate the responsibility for choosing
your trading points to your ten year old fifth grader, who doubtless
has an adequate math background by now to keep you "straight" on the
orders you should be placing for your trading account!

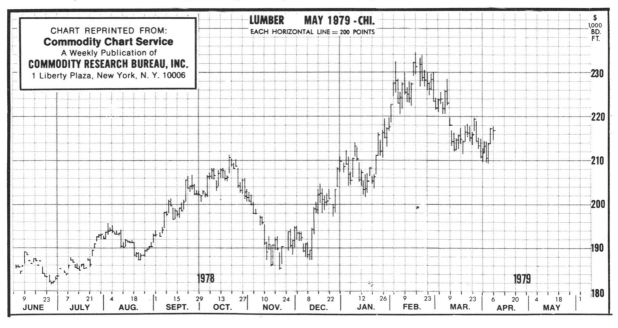

CHART REPRINTED FROM:
Commodity Chart Service
A Weekly Publication of
COMMODITY RESEARCH BUREAU, INC.
1 Liberty Plaza, New York, N. Y. 10006

LUMBER   MAY 1979 -CHI.
EACH HORIZONTAL LINE = 200 POINTS

The precise midpoint of the Nov-Feb move from 185.00 to 234.20 is
at 209.6. Note the substantial support developing at that exact
level as this book is being written!

Too Bad PEPS Isn't PEEPS!

Be sure to view the PEPS system in perspective for what it is-
a system for timing trade entry. (Another alternative title I considered
for this book was "Precision Bid Commodity Trading"). The system does a
fantastic job of getting us into the market at, or near, the extreme
point of reactions. Getting out of the trade is another matter entirely,
and is not relevant to the study I have conducted into the percentage
extent of reactions. I have been discussing PEPS with my clients for over
a year. One witty trader quickly realized the major shortcoming of PEPS,
that of not telling us where to exit the market. Upon learning the name
I had given this system, PEPS, he waxed waggish (forgive me!), remarking
"Too bad PEPS isn't PEEPS". He clarified his point:

   PEPS = Precise Entry Point System
   PEEPS = Precise Entry and Exit Point System

   Although the major portion of the research I have conducted centers
around the range of percentages most commonly achieved during reactionary
phases, I have developed several methods of how best to deal with the problem of how best to exit a trade once entered using the PEPS system.

   Empirical observation has shown me that one phenomenon frequently
seen is a sharp, sudden move in favor of trades entered using PEPS. Now,
perhaps with roughly equal distribution, some of these trades will lead
to major profit potential, and some will lead only to minor, temporary
profits which will quickly evaporate if not taken. Two situations which
will serve to illustrate this observation graphically are:

Major
profit
potential

50%

50%

Minor
profit
potential

In the first instance pictured above, the validity of the trade was never in question as the market continued moving in the hoped-for direction (up). In the second situation, although the 50% level eventually gave way and would have led to a loss if the trade were held until the 66% stop was elected, there was, first, a characteristic sharp "bounce" from this level.

I have found no reliable method of determining in advance which of these two possibilities will emerge in any given trade. However, I have found a method very useful in dealing with this problem. As soon as the reaction has met support (resistance) and "bounced", take out your initial stop at the 66% level, and raise (lower) it to a level that would assure no loss on the trade. This I refer to as a "free ride stop". We are now in the market at or very near the bottom (top) of a reaction, with a no-loss trade "locked up". If the market resumes its reactionary phase, we are out of the trade at no loss. If it successfully resumes the previous (up)trend, we are "on board" and in position to capitalize on a major profit opportunity.

A variation of the above technique that may prove more pragmatic might be to put our stop just under the low (over the high) achieved on the reaction rather than the "free ride stop". This keeps us in the market on the occasions when the market "tests" the reaction low (high) before resuming the original trend direction, and our "free ride stop" would have been hit. The additional risk assumed is slight, and the frequency with which the reaction will test the extreme level without penetrating it is great enough, in my opinion, to warrant the small additional risk entailed by using this technique.

50%
Set stop just
below reaction
low

Set stop just over
reaction high
50%

As mentioned before, trade <u>exit</u> is not the forté of this system. Traditional techniques of determining price objectives may be considered as a means of setting profit taking objectives. Two concepts with which you should familiarize yourself in this regard are the principle of the Elliott Wave, and the concept of the "measured move".

Elliott Wave theory can become rather complex, if studied in detail, but the main point of the theory is that most major price moves can be observed to consist of three main price moves in the major trend direction, corrected by two counter waves, or reactionary phases. These reactions are observed as often consisting of an A-B-C configuration:

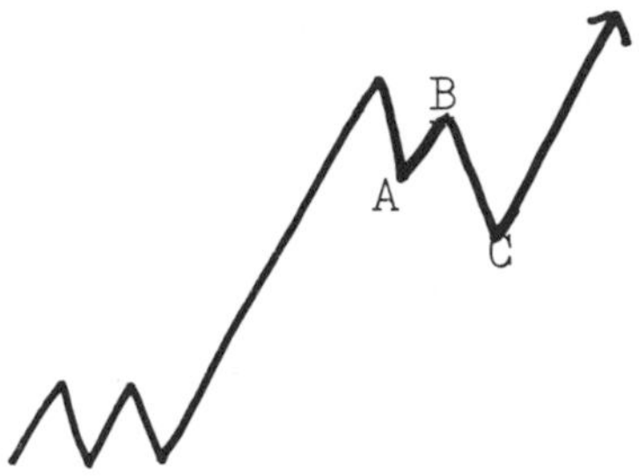

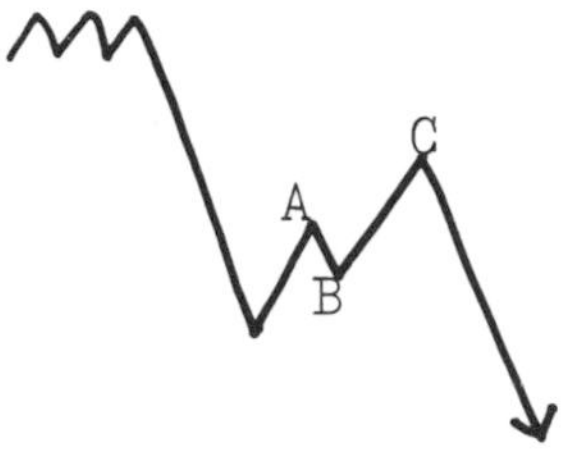

The overall picture of a major price trend, when completed, would appear roughly as illustrated below:

I find that in utilizing the above theory, it is prudent to assume that it is much safer to buy (sell) the <u>first</u> or the <u>second</u> 50% reaction within the trend than subsequent ones. The assumption is that the <u>third</u> or later reaction within a major trend is far more likely to be a <u>trend</u> <u>reversal</u> than are earlier reactions.

In such a case, I would consider the likely possibility that the entire major trend may be corrected by approximately 50% at which level I would look for the market to meet support.

LOC = Life of Contract

Utilizing the "measured move" concept may prove useful in establishing profit-taking objectives. This concept deals with the empirical observation that the length or extent of any given "leg" within a given price trend will often approximate the length (extent) of the preceding leg, as measured from the extreme of the reaction following the leg.

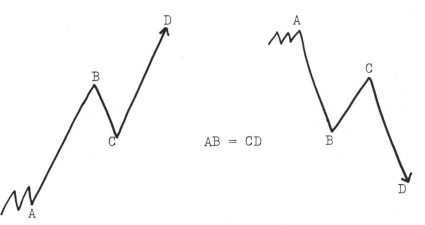

AB = CD

In both cases above, the extent of move CD would be expected to approximate the extent of move AB. Watch closely for support (resistance) at the level projected in this manner, and be prepared to bank profits quickly if a reaction begins to set in. Then, use the PEPS system to pinpoint a good <u>reentry</u> level at which to reestablish your position, with appropriate protective stops should the reaction take on more than "normal" proportions.

The chart of May 1978 wheat below will serve to illustrate this principle.

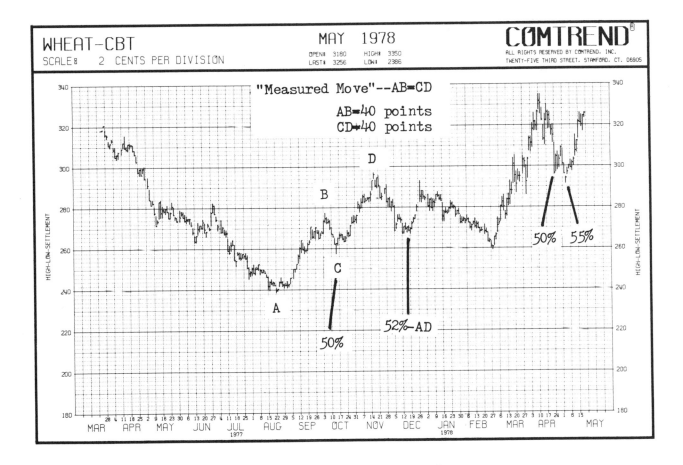

OK, So It Works...But Why?

As stated elsewhere in this book, I don't think it really
matters, from a pragmatic viewpoint, why reactions approximate
50% with such consistency. But from an intellectual viewpoint,
I think it would be most desirable to understand the underlying
rationale. I'm sorry to report that my research into the very
limited literature and references available on this phenomenon
doesn't really give much of a clue.

However, some writers have made relevant comments which
I feel are worth quoting here.

Burton H Pugh, in his Trader's Instruction Book, makes
several observations concerning the 50% reaction specifically,
and concerning market behavior in general (which is caused, in
the aggregate, by the actions of all market participants). I have
personally always viewed commodity trading as a vast, continuous
financial chess game, in which each player is pitted against the
skills and knowledge (or lack thereof) of all the other players.
On a nearly continuous basis, old players drop out as their lack
of knowledge or trading talent cause them to be "checkmated", and
new players, eagerly seeking the substantial profits that accrue
to the winners, move in to take their place. The market ("THEY")
is a highly skilled, omniscient opponent, and we, the players, need
all the knowledge of our opponent's habits, characteristic behavior
traits, and thought processes we can possibly learn. That is why a
thorough awareness of the market's tendency to react by fifty per-
cent is so vital...it is one of our "opponent's" most predictable
habits.

The players in the market themselves have characteristic
behavior patterns which, in turn, produce the patterns of market
behavior which we can readily observe.

As Pugh tells us, "The forecaster must be able to measure and
forecast the conduct of the human element in the market. Because men

have habits the market has habits and because human nature does not greatly change you will find market habits running along about the same year after year."

Joseph Granville, in his book <u>Granville's</u> <u>New</u> <u>Strategy</u> <u>of</u> <u>Daily</u> <u>Stock</u> <u>Market</u> <u>Timing</u> <u>For</u> <u>Maximum</u> <u>Profit</u>, also comments on the underlying rationale behind the importance of the 50% level: "The theory is very logical, best explained in terms of the physical movement of the seesaw. A seesaw is in equilibrium at the 50% level, perfectly horizontal. Once that equilibrium is disturbed and one half of the seesaw goes above the 50% level, it will then keep going all the way as far as it can. The other half of the seesaw will make a compensating movement in the opposite direction, going as far as it can. The market application of the Principle states that if a market decline retraces more than 50% of the advance, then the entire advance is likely to be wiped out. Conversely, if the market retraces more than 50% of a decline, the theory holds that the entire decline will be retraced. <u>Retracements</u> of less than 50% would indicate that the original movement is still in force."

To revert to Pugh's comments:"This is one of the most valuable market habits. Every swing either up or down will soon or late be followed by a reversal of the market of half the distance covered by the swing. If wheat rallies twenty cents, it will decline ten cents. The decline may be much more than ten cents, but you can be sure of the ten. ...Nearly all of the small rallies and reactions of the day show the same habit."

Still later, in his work <u>Trader's</u> <u>Instruction</u> <u>Book</u> Pugh refers to the 50% reaction as one of the ten famous "market keys" to understanding the market. "This is probably the most commonly known of the ten keys. It is especially valuable in mild bull or bear markets as such markets work up or down by orderly steps. In the advancing market shown in wheat and Studebaker the market makes about a normal upswing then drops back approximately 50 per cent of the upturn. This reaction may vary from 40% to 60% but is near enough to 50% to base your estimates on that figure. If you...determined that top had been

made for a decline to come, this key would show you where
to expect a halt and the upward move begin again. You would
take profits when the market showed 'top' and repurchase 50
per cent down for another upswing.

These 50 per cent reactions are caused by many of the
smaller traders taking profits and waiting for this reaction
to 'buy in' again. ...

On declines both in grains and stocks the same process
takes place with rallies of 50 per cent. ...Finally the reaction
will about equal or fully equal the upswing. This indicates top
has been made and the decline is in progress. The same holds
good for the movements near bottom. When rallies equal the down-
swing, bottom has been made."

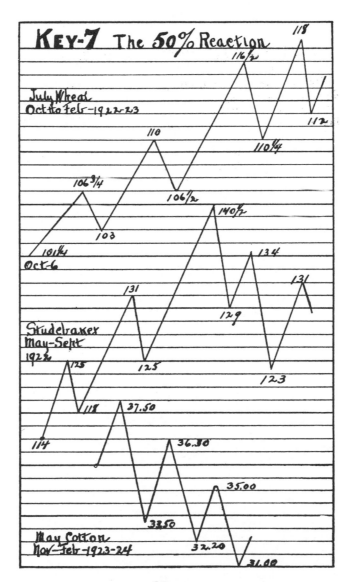

I am grateful to my friend, Billy Jones, for his permission to reprint the above material from Pugh's works. Billy's company, Lambert-Gann Publishing Co., Box O, Pomeroy, WA 99347 has reprinted and again made available all of the market writings of Gann and Pugh, which were out of print and unavailable for many years.

With the kind permission of Mr. Chester Keltner, of Keltner Statistical Service, 1004 Baltimore Ave., Kansas City, MO 64105, I am reprinting the following relevant material from his book, How To Make Money In Commodities.

The Theory of Action and Reaction

The technical market student is concerned first of all, or at least should be, with price trend. To be a successful trader he must know at all times the direction of the price trend and his position in the market must be kept in harmony with it. A trader attempting to take advantage of daily trend movements, for example, should never be short when the daily trend is up, and he should never be long when the daily trend is down. Likewise, a minor trend trader should never be short when the minor trend is up, and he should never be long when the minor trend is down. Not all traders will use the same methods for determining these trends but the important point is that irrespective of the method used a cardinal rule of the technical market student is that his position in the market must always be in harmony with the trend on which he is trading.

This does not mean, however, that the technical student is prevented from making against-the-trend purchases and sales on price swings that occur within the trend on which he is trading. It is in connection with these against-the-trend purchases and sales that a knowledge of the theory of action and reaction is important.

A characteristic of markets is that they fluctuate. These fluctuations do not occur in a set, precise pattern. But they do tend to have certain general characterstics, and it is these general characterstics that provide the basis for the theory of action and reaction. The theory is that a reaction in an advancing market should retrace roughly one-half of the previous advance. Also, a rally in a declining market should retrace roughly one-half of the previous decline. There is of course no way of knowing just when these correctionary moves will occur. The object, therefore, is not to predict them but rather to take advantage of them when they occur. *

In the accompanying chart I show a theoretical market which perfectly illustrates the theory of action and reaction. In the overall advance from A to F there are two correctionary reactions (from B to C and from D to E), each retracing exactly one-half of the previous move. I should point out also that the advance from A to F is in three stages, which is a pattern that is considered typical of a normal bull move. The first stage of the overall advance was from A to B, the second stage from C to D and the third and final stage from E to F. I personally don't think one should accept too literally this concept that a bull move must always occur in three stages. I have seen bull moves end after only one or two stages of advance, but I would concede at least that after three stages have occurred there is added reason for suspecting that a bull move may have run its course.

Referring again to the action and reaction chart, you will note that in the advance from G to H exactly one-half of the decline from F to G was retraced. At H the trader could not be certain that the bull move had been completed. But when (after retracing one-half of the decline from F to G) the market dropped below G, this indicated the trend

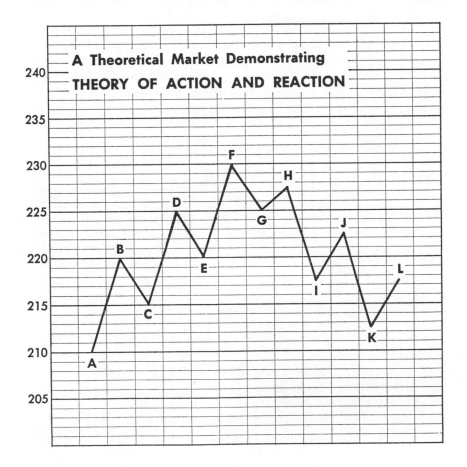

A Theoretical Market Demonstrating THEORY OF ACTION AND REACTION

Trading pattern.

had turned down. Because three completed stages of advance had occurred, it is possible that a trader would have sold out his long position or at least have lightened his commitment when the market hesitated at H and could not get above that point. In any event, he would have sold out and gone short when the market sold below G. He then might have added to his short position with against-the-trend sales at J and L.

It should be emphasized of course that retracement (or correctionary) moves in actual markets are not always exactly one-half retracements. They can fall anywhere within the one-third to two-thirds area and not violate in any way the theory of action and reaction. The tendency, actually, is for retracement moves to be less than 50% in markets under the domination of either extremely bullish or bearish influences. In markets in which the bullish and bearish factors are in relatively even balance, retracement moves tend to be in excess of 50% of the previous move.

Under the theory of action and reaction there is another rule that should be noted. It is that in an advancing market each stage of advance will tend to be equal to the previous advance, and in a declining market each stage of decline will also tend to be equal to the previous decline. You will note in the action and reaction chart that the advances from A to B, from C to D and from E to F are all equal. The decline from F to G is less than the decline from H to I, but the declines from H to I and J to K are equal. Again in this instance, the rule is not a precise one. In fact, in a normal bull market I would say that the stages of advance should tend to become broader, with the broadest move of all coming during the final phase of the bull market. In a normal bear market the tendency should be just the reverse.

You may recall that I previously said there is no way of knowing just when a retracement move will occur. This is of course true. But on the basis of the rule which says that in a bull market each stage of advance should be roughly equal to the previous one and also that in a bear market each stage of decline should be roughly equal to the previous decline you do at least have a way of approximating where advances and declines will terminate. On the basis of this rule, the technical market student can frequently

43

accept profits against the trend to good advantage on trades that are made in harmony with the trend movement.

In order to observe how the theory of action and re-action usually works, and how it is possible to make profit-able against-the-trend purchases and sales on price swings that occur within the limits of a particular price trend, I suggest that you refer to the May wheat and May soybean price charts at the back of the book showing the daily high, low and closing prices for these futures for the past ten years. You do not have to study these price patterns at any great length to note that the theory of action and reaction is an exceedingly sound theory and that a knowledge of it can be highly profitable to the trader who develops an ability to objectively analyze price movements.

Mr. Keltner's book has a fine collection of charts which should prove quite useful in analyzing the reaction percentages in past years' charts. Traders Press also has a book available, Commodities: A Chart Anthology, which provides over 1,000 completed life-of-contract bar charts dating back to 1960 and which should prove quite useful for historical research purposes.

Will Too Many Cooks Spoil The Broth?

In market vernacular, will the publicity this book accords the phenomenon of the 50% reaction lead to its demise as a viable timing tool? In my opinion, the answer is a resounding NO!, or I would never have published this book. I have had lengthy conversations with Charley Ballentine about this question, and we both concur on the above conclusion. I don't think any pattern of market behavior as well-entrenched and as long enduring can be changed by a bit of publicity. Perhaps temporarily, as many traders "try their hand" at using this system...but eventually, the rule should continue to work.

Technical analysis, as a means of market timing, has become very popular in the last 15 or 20 years. I have seen one professional trader say he doesn't "believe" in charts, but he does keep them so he will know what people who do believe in them are doing. Critics of this method call it "self-fulfilling prophecy". They point out that when large numbers of traders are all playing by the same ground rules, and watching the same charts, that their concerted, unified buying and selling will produce the very results their charts are predicting. They contend it is their selling when prices break the neckline of a head and shoulders top that causes the next move to be down; their profit taking (buying) in expectation of the "return move" to the neckline that leads to the expected return move rally; their renewed selling after such rally that turns the market back down, etc.,etc. All in all, it is nothing but self-fulfilling prophecy, they say.

To me, this argument, though seemingly logical, is bunk. For technical analysis and trading are nothing more than the _pragmatic_ _application_ of what has been _empirically_ _observed_ to be _consistently_ _repetitive_ market behavior. Try to explain away the fact that charts of markets 25, 50, even 100 years ago show much the same formations and behavioral habits that they do today...and this was at a time when most market participants knew little, if anything, about the now-popular charting techniques. _Why_ these phenomena (trendlines, heads and shoulders, 50% retracements, etc.) work is not really important to me. The fact that they _do_ _work_ with enough consistency to be used profitably is vitally important to me.

I've never seen a price chart of the daily fluctuations in the price of tulip bulbs in Holland during the famous speculative spree hundreds of years ago. Indeed, one probably does not even exist. But, if one were in existence, I feel confident it would exhibit many of the market phenomena and habits we technicians take note of in runaway upside moves and subsequent reversals today. I'll bet there would be a "measuring gap" halfway up the move, that any reactions on the way to the top in tulip bulb prices approximated 50%, and that the top day may well have consisted of a "key reversal". All this centuries before charting became popular as a means of market analysis, yet the same characteristics of market behavior endure today.

No, I don't think the 50% reaction will disappear just because my book may help to popularize the utilization of this phenomenon. W.D. Gann has been dead nearly a quarter of a century now, and his observation about the validity of the 50% retracement is still as valid as ever. And I'll bet that long after I've left the commodity arena (I hope to have many years left to play the game, yet!) future readers of this book, many years from now, will say: "You mean it worked so well as long ago as 1979, and it is still working so well _now_?"

SO YOU THINK IT'S ONLY 20/20 HINDSIGHT?

I will readily grant that in many cases fifty per cent reactions are more readily discernible when viewed after the fact with the advantage of 20/20 hindsight. However, learning what price levels are <u>likely</u> to offer support or resistance based on this principle and learning to <u>anticipate</u> these levels <u>in advance</u> is the key to it's successful use.

I am confident that after reading this book, if you will conscientiously <u>watch</u> <u>reactions</u> as they evolve, calculate the level at which they should terminate, then observe the remarkable frequency with which they halt near the 50% level, you will, in due course, come to believe that you are the proud possessor of 20/20 foresight!

<u>HELP</u>!

Not possessing any personal knowledge whatever of computer technology, nor the <u>savoir faire</u> to even explain the parameters that should be observed in performing a computer assisted study of the effectiveness of the PEPS system, I have been frustrated in my desire to obtain the results of such a study.

Perhaps the principle is too subjective in terms of which points to use as measuring levels for any meaningful objective study to be made. I don't feel capable of making this determination myself however, and want to appeal to those among my audience who feel qualified and who have the wherewithal to do so to undertake a study of the effectiveness of the PEPS system. I would be most grateful for, and interested in seeing the results of such a study.

I have chosen the 45%/50%/55%/66% levels of the PEPS system on a purely subjective basis, as a result of the empirical observation of what appeared to be the most effective levels. Perhaps such a study might divulge other points that work more effectively.

Another area I would love to see covered is that of <u>documenting</u> the effectiveness of PEPS via an actual, real-life trading account devoted to implementing the principles of PEPS. In my estimation, such an account would need to be of adequate size to diversify "across the board", and to trade halfway levels in whatever markets they became available in. If any readers would have an interest in doing so, I would be delighted to collaborate with them in trading a PEPS account. I may be contacted through TRADERS PRESS if you have an interest in working with me.

RECOMMENDED READING

The books listed below represent selected titles published by TRADERS PRESS, INC, and should be of interest to the stock or commodity trader. Each of these books, as well as many others on stock and commodity trading, is available through TRADERS PRESS. Please write P.O. Box 10344 Greenville, S C 29603 if you would like to order any of the books listed here, or if you would like a free copy of the TRADERS PRESS TRADERS CATALOGUE, which lists and describes over one hundred books of interest to traders.

COMMODITIES: A CHART ANTHOLOGY by Edward Dobson. An extensive collection of over 1,100 completed daily life-of-contract bar charts covers most major markets during the twenty year period 1960-1980. A great research tool for researching PEPS, seasonality, pattern recognition analysis, or any other system.

REMINISCENCES OF A STOCK OPERATOR by Edwin Lefevre. My personal favorite book. The most highly sought after book ever written on Wall Street lore, this book is the fictionalized biography of Jesse Livermore, the colorful speculator of yesteryear. Belongs in every trader's library.

COMMODITY SPREADS: A HISTORICAL CHART PERSPECTIVE by Edward Dobson. Pure and simple: if you trade spreads, or are considering them, this book is an indispensable reference. Has been referred to as "The Spreader's Bible".

JESSE LIVERMORE: SPECULATOR KING by Paul Sarnoff. An actual biography of Livermore, the Boy Plunger, the Great Bear, the Cotton King. Fascinating reading about one of America's most colorful and flamboyant speculators.

UNDERSTANDING FIBONACCI NUMBERS by Edward Dobson. A primer booklet explaining Fibonacci concepts, numbers, and relationships. Interesting reading on a most fascinating subject.

ACKNOWLEDGEMENT

The following charts are reprinted from two sources which I would like to recognize:

The Comtrend charts are reprinted from the pages of COMMODITIES: A CHART ANTHOLOGY, a publication of TRADERS PRESS, INC. The charts in it are, in turn, reprinted with the permission of Comtrend, Twenty Five Third Street, Stamford, CT 06905.

The full-size charts are reprinted with the permission of Commodity Perspective, 30 South Wacker Drive, Suite 1220, Chicago, IL 60606.

Finally, I would like to thank my friends at Commodity Research Bureau, 75 Montgomery Street, Jersey City, N J 07302 for the use of their charts, which are used in previous sections of the book.

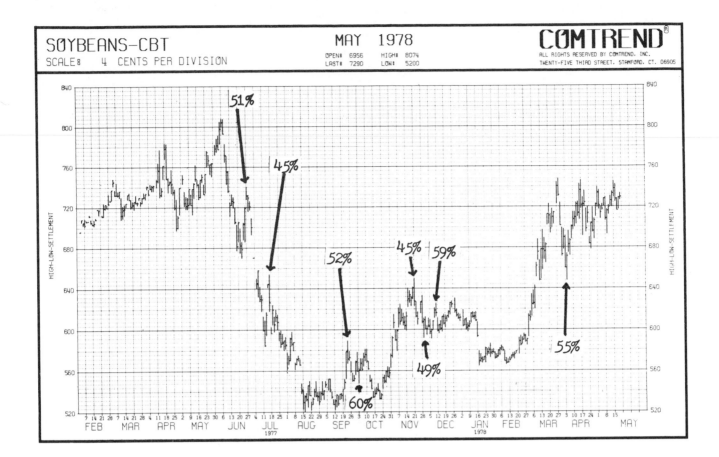

SOYBEANS–CBT   MAY 1978   COMTREND®

SCALE: 4 CENTS PER DIVISION

OPEN# 6956   HIGH# 8074
LAST# 7290   LOW# 5200

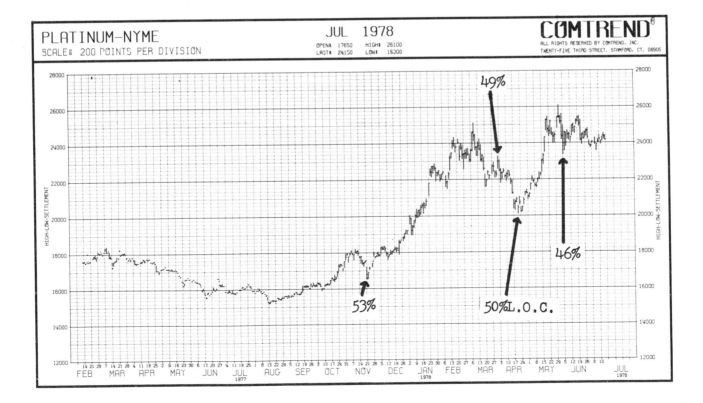

PLATINUM–NYME   JUL 1978   COMTREND®

SCALE: 200 POINTS PER DIVISION

OPEN# 17650   HIGH# 26100
LAST# 24150   LOW# 15200

51

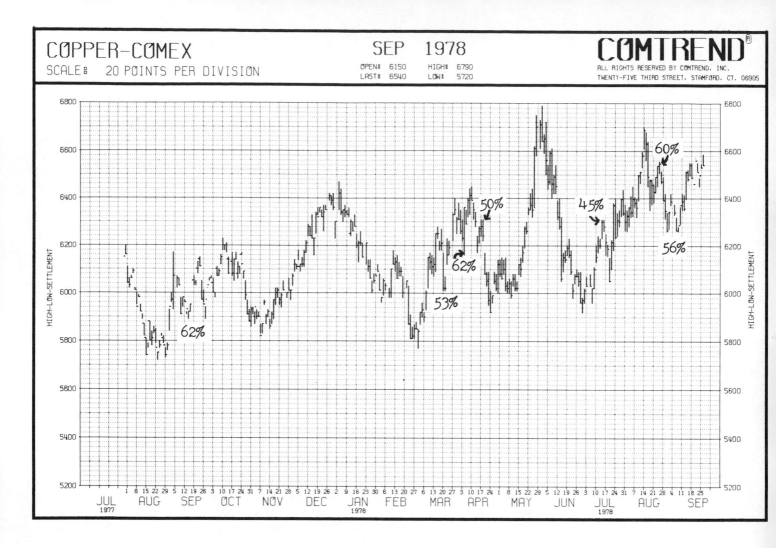

COPPER-COMEX SEP 1978 COMTREND
SCALE: 20 POINTS PER DIVISION
OPEN: 6150 HIGH: 6790
LAST: 6540 LOW: 5720

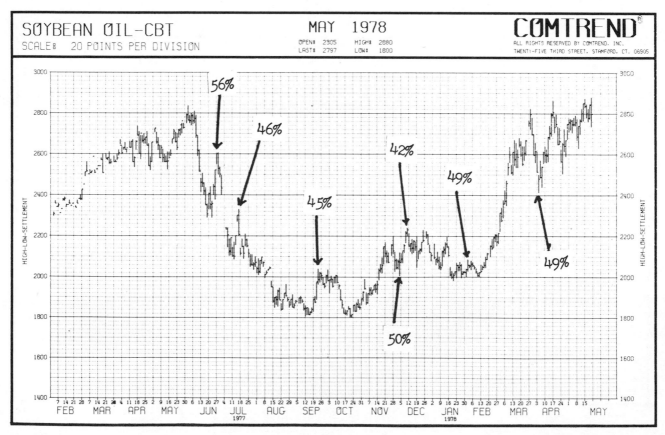

SOYBEAN OIL-CBT MAY 1978 COMTREND
SCALE: 20 POINTS PER DIVISION
OPEN: 2305 HIGH: 2880
LAST: 2797 LOW: 1800

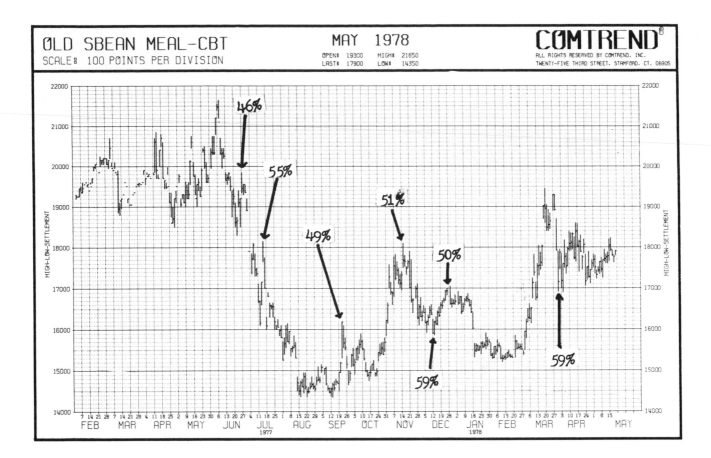

OLD SBEAN MEAL-CBT
SCALE: 100 POINTS PER DIVISION
MAY 1978
OPEN: 19300 HIGH: 21650
LAST: 17900 LOW: 14350
COMTREND

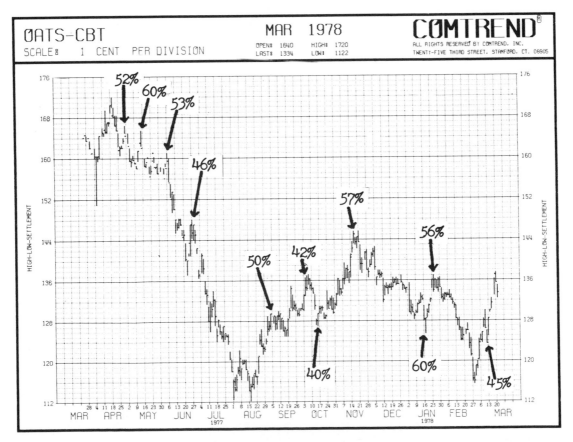

OATS-CBT
SCALE: 1 CENT PER DIVISION
MAR 1978
OPEN: 1640 HIGH: 1720
LAST: 1334 LOW: 1122
COMTREND

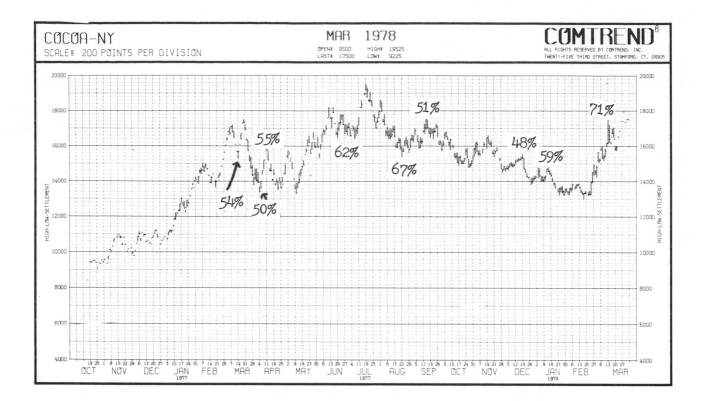

COCOA-NY   MAR 1978   COMTREND®
SCALE: 200 POINTS PER DIVISION
OPEN: 9500   HIGH: 19525
LAST: 17500   LOW: 9225

LIVE CATTLE-NEW   FEB 1978   COMTREND®
SCALE: 20 POINTS PER DIVISION
OPEN: 4300   HIGH: 4725
LAST: 4702   LOW: 3615

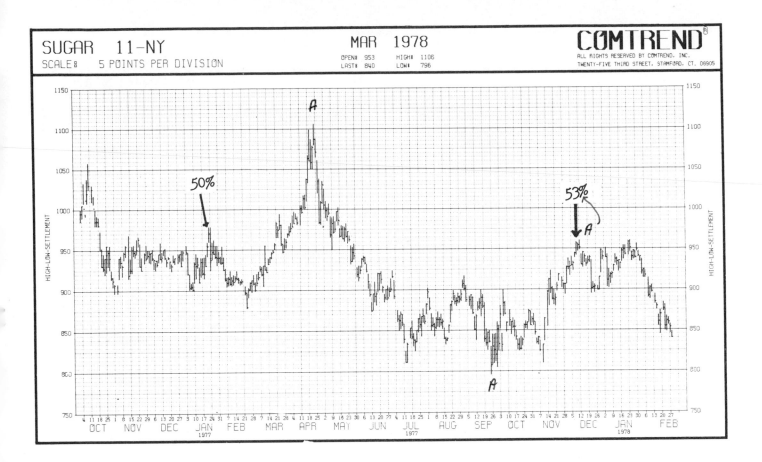

Note how an awareness of the importance of the 50% level might keep you <u>out</u> <u>of trouble</u>... When sugar broke out of its base over 900 in November, the market appeared to have completed a major base, and accomplished a major trend reversal. Note how potent the 50% level was in stopping the newly established uptrend!

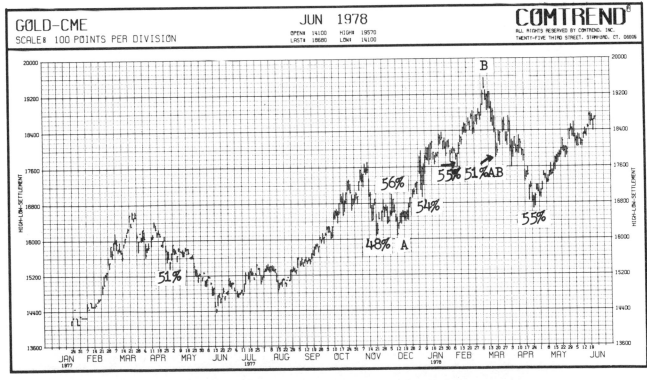

PØRK BELLIES-CME   FEB 1978   COMTREND®

SCALE: 50 POINTS PER DIVISION

OPEN# 4800   HIGH# 7397
LAST# 6912   LOW# 4350

ALL RIGHTS RESERVED BY COMTREND, INC.
TWENTY-FIVE THIRD STREET, STAMFORD, CT. 06905

49%
50%
63%
60%
48%
55% 56%
56%

OCT NOV DEC JAN FEB MAR APR MAY JUN JUL AUG SEP OCT NOV DEC JAN FEB
1977   1977   1978

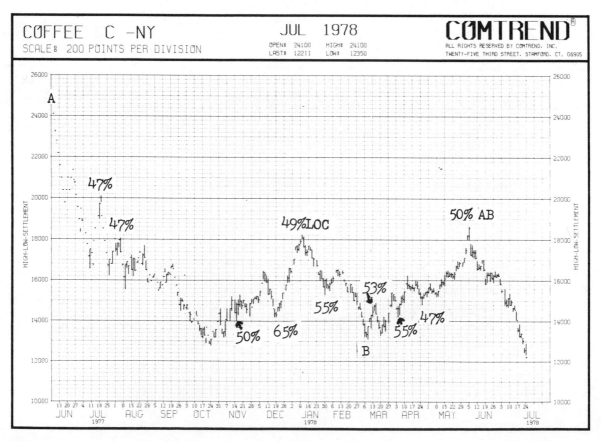

CØFFEE C -NY   JUL 1978   COMTREND®

SCALE: 200 POINTS PER DIVISION

OPEN# 24100   HIGH# 24100
LAST# 12211   LOW# 12350

ALL RIGHTS RESERVED BY COMTREND, INC.
TWENTY-FIVE THIRD STREET, STAMFORD, CT. 06905

A
47%
47%
49%LOC
50% AB
53%
55%
50% 65%
55% 47%
B

JUN JUL AUG SEP OCT NOV DEC JAN FEB MAR APR MAY JUN JUL
    1977   1978   1978

56

PØRK BELLIES-CME JUL 1978 COMTREND®
SCALE: 100 POINTS PER DIVISION OPEN: 5475 HIGH: 8575
LAST: 5050 LOW: 4450
ALL RIGHTS RESERVED BY COMTREND, INC.
TWENTY-FIVE THIRD STREET, STAMFORD, CT. 06905

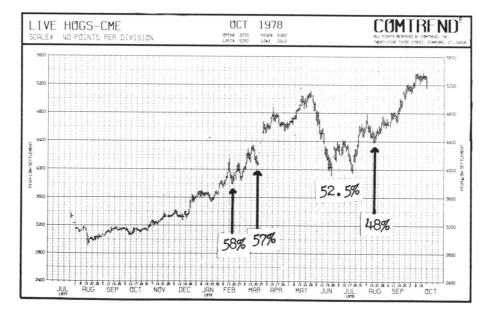

LIVE HØGS-CME OCT 1978 COMTREND®
SCALE: 40 POINTS PER DIVISION OPEN: 3370 HIGH: 5380
LAST: 5250 LOW: 2910
ALL RIGHTS RESERVED BY COMTREND, INC.
TWENTY-FIVE THIRD STREET, STAMFORD, CT. 06905

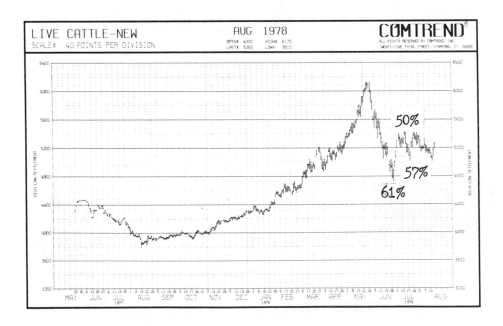

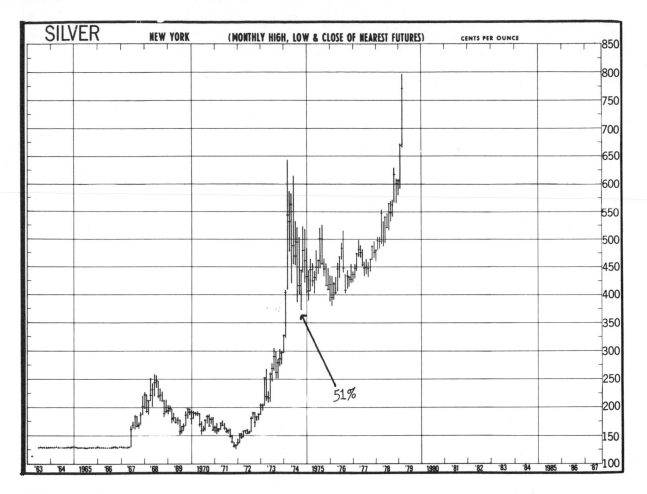

SILVER   NEW YORK   (MONTHLY HIGH, LOW & CLOSE OF NEAREST FUTURES)   CENTS PER OUNCE

Although my analysis and discussion of the 50% phenomenon have centered
exclusively around the daily bar chart, you will find that it is often
found in longer term charts, as depicted here in the long term price
trends of silver and gold.

GOLD   CASH PRICE   LONDON

DOLLARS PER OUNCE

WEEKLY HIGH, LOW & CLOSE (BASED ON DAILY EARLY & AFTERNOON QUOTE)

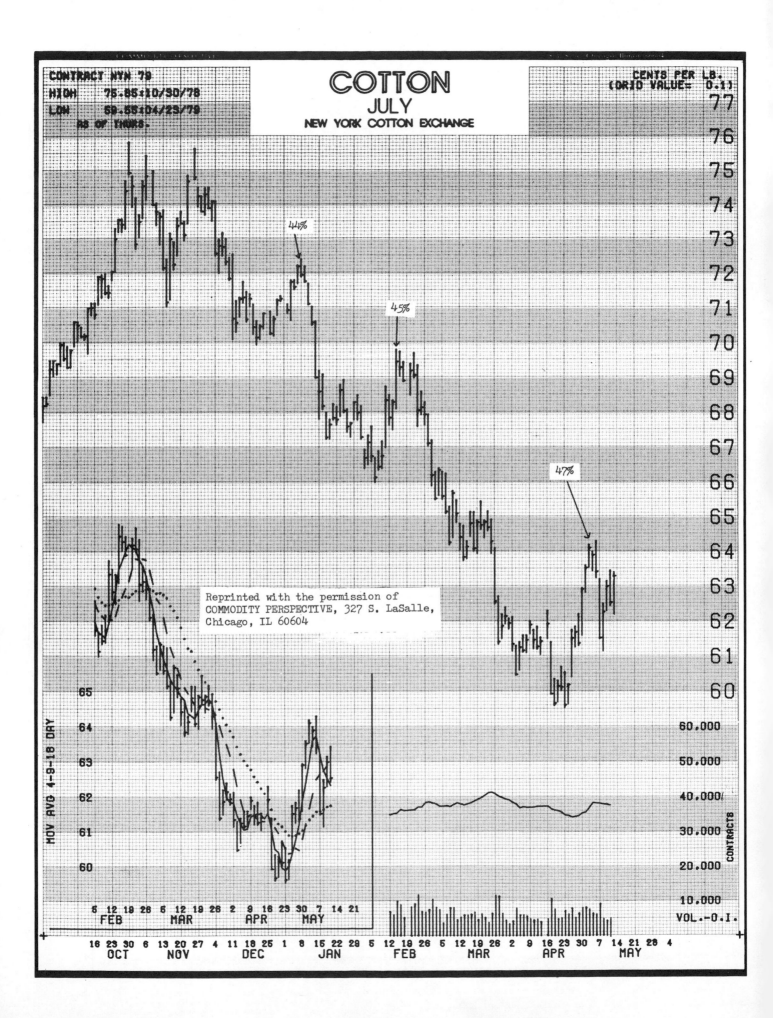

COTTON
JULY
NEW YORK COTTON EXCHANGE

CONTRACT NYM 79
HIGH   75.85±10/30/78
LOW   59.55±04/25/79
          AS OF THURS.

CENTS PER LB.
(GRID VALUE= 0.1)

44%

45%

47%

Reprinted with the permission of
COMMODITY PERSPECTIVE, 327 S. LaSalle,
Chicago, IL 60604

MOV AVG 4-9-18 DAY

VOL.-O.I.

CONTRACTS

Postscript: (Added May 22, 1979)

The front cover of this book depicts the May 1979 lumber contract. In the text of the book, the chart of this contract was included as it was trading in the 209.5-214 level with the comment that the market was receiving support at the major halfway level that halved the move from 185 to 234.2. I thought the ensuing development was quite noteworthy, and am including the chart of the completed contract here.

The back cover of the book shows us June 1979 IMM Gold. As the chart depicts, the market had just broken out of a major head and shoulders top at the time the material was being prepared for the book, indicating a minimum downside target of 225. Note how the decline stopped precisely at 231.5 (and closed that day at 233.0), almost precisely at the 50% level. The ensuing rally, which at first appeared to be the well-known "return move" to the neckline, has developed into a full-fledged resumption of the major uptrend, leading to new contract highs. Thus, the 50% level proved even more potent than the measuring implications of the head and shoulders pattern, widely known as one of the most reliable bar chart formations.

ADDENDUM TO SECOND PRINTING

(Written September 4, 1985)

This addendum to the first printing of THE TRADING RULE THAT CAN MAKE YOU RICH* is written in September, 1985, almost seven years after the original material was written. Here I will share with you additional observations on characteristic market behavior during corrective retracements which I have noticed during this period.

First, and foremost, the 50% phenomenon still works! During the years since this book was written, I have seen this principle continue to occur with great regularity, thereby reinforcing and corroborating my belief in it more than ever. The most recent standout example of this is seen in the daily chart of March 1986 Sugar, where an explosive upmove from 333 to 559 was followed by an almost precise 50% retracement to 441. Anyone who had followed the principles espoused in THE TRADING RULE... and bought at the 446 halfway point was immediately rewarded by explosion to new highs for the move, with a subsequent high of 585 being acheived the day these words are written.

During this seven year period I have learned of many other approaches to technical analysis with which I was not familiar in 1979, such as Fibonacci ratios, cycle analysis, and the use of technical indicators such as RSI, MACD (Moving Average Convergence-Divergence), oscillators, etc. Many of these tools and indicators are quite useful, especially with respect to short term trading, yet I feel that I have not yet encountered any timing device more effective, in my opinion, than the 50% level!

Another point I would like to emphasize is that this principle seems to work not only on longer term periods as measured by daily, weekly, or monthly charts, but on a very short term basis as well. Since I began working with an intraday graphics system earlier this year (May 1985), it has become apparent to me (whereas it was not before I had access to short term data) that the 50% retracement occurs often on very short term price movements. This is evident on price charts using increments as small as 2 minutes per bar, as well as on 5, 10, 15, 30 minute charts, and on hourly charts, all of which I now utilize in my trading. These retracements are usually not evident on daily bar charts. For the short term trader, this is indispensable knowledge.

As a note of interest to those who may be interested in investigating the use of an intraday graphics service, I have been most pleased with the system I have chosen, which utilizes TRADEPLAN software which is developed by CompuTrac. The system uses a high resolution color monitor, and the charts may be printed in color using a Canon PJ-1080A printer, which is available from CompuTrac. I would strongly recommend this excellent system to anyone interested in short term technical analysis, and would encourage you to contact Mr. Tim Slater at CompuTrac, 1021 9th Street, New Orleans, LA 70115 for additional information. I would also be glad to discuss this with you if you will forward your name and daytime phone number to me at P.O. Box 10344, Greenville, S C 29603.

In 1979, when I wrote THE TRADING RULE..., I was only vaguely familiar with the term Fibonacci. I have since become substantially more familiar with this concept and its 38.2% and 61.8% retracements. (See my booklet, UNDERSTANDING FIBONACCI NUMBERS, published by TRADERS PRESS, for additional information). Examination of price charts will indeed divulge many retracements of almost these exact proportions. One thing I have noticed is that a very strong price move will retrace only 38%, and a weaker move will retrace the full 62%. I have also noticed that many times an ABC correction will retrace 38% on the

"A" leg, and the "C" leg will extend to the 50% level.

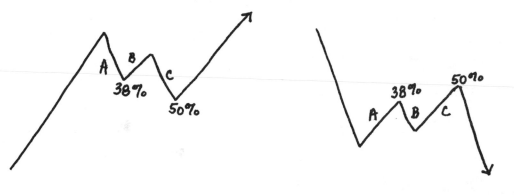

On corrective moves that <u>exceed</u> the 50% level, you will often see

the A leg go to 50%, then the C leg subsequently go to 62%.

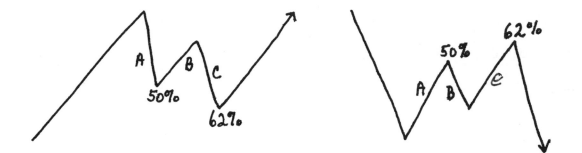

Far less frequently, you will see a five wave correction which

carries to the 38%, 50%, and 62% levels on successive legs of the correction.

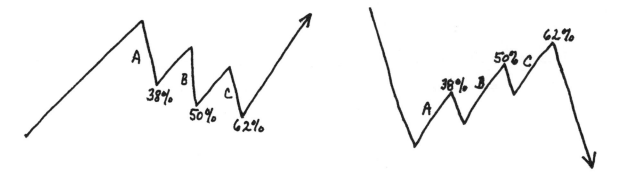

Another observation I would like to share with you concerns the

<u>quality</u> of the retracement. As I have heard my friend John Hill say, "It

is not what the market <u>does</u>, but <u>how it does it</u> that is important." If I

am considering buying a 50% retracement following an upmove, I have noticed
that this will be far more likely to produce a good trade if the retracement
takes place gradually, if the market must slowly work its way down, than if it
quickly and easily collapses to the 50% level. Quite often, a fast 50% decline
will be followed by a brief rally, then additional weakness ensues, often
leading to a full retracement of the move up, even a move down to new lows.
A gradual 50% retracement is more likely to be followed by a move to new highs.
This applies in reverse to corrections of downmoves. It goes without saying
that these observations apply to many cases I have observed, but not all. I
view commodity trading as being similar in some respects to playing bridge:
the underlying principles remain the same, but each hand is different!

A fast, easily accomplished 50%
retracement is often followed
by a full retracement.

A gradual retracement is more
likely to offer a good entry point
which leads to a resumption of the
main move.

After reading my book years ago, Larry Williams wrote me and called
to my attention a very interesting concept: often one will see a 50% correction
in terms of time consumed by the move. That is, an upmove which takes place
over twenty time periods (daily, hourly, weekly, etc.) will tend to be followed
by a correction which consumes ten time periods before the original move resumes.

This is a most interesting concept, however I have done no research to verify it.I would welcome comments from any reader who can share his own observations on this relationship.

It is my chosen career to work as an account executive with a major NYSE brokerage firm, working with individual traders in the handling of their accounts. I have been a trader for my own account since 1966, and have been a broker since 1970. Should you find yourself in a situation where your own brokerage affiliation is not proving satisfactory, and you would like to consider working with a broker of twenty years experience, I would welcome hearing from you through TRADERS PRESS, P.O. Box 10344, Greenville, S C 29603. I constantly monitor the active markets seeking trading opportunities of the type described in this book, and those using other methods I have found to be reliable as well (for instance I have recently begun working with MACD, moving average convergence-divergence lines, with great success). Please forward your name and daytime phone. I'll give you a call to see if our "chemistry" is right to work together.

To each of you, I take this opportunity to wish you the best of luck and success in all your future trading endeavors. As my friend Bo Thunman says, "May the Trend Be With You!".

Edward D. Dobson

Edward D. Dobson
Greenville, SC
September 4, 1985

TRADER'S PRESS, INC.
P.O. BOX 10344
GREENVILLE, S.C. 29603

BOOKS FOR STOCK
AND COMMODITY
TRADERS

We have in stock most of the titles of interest to the technically oriented trader, as well as many other books of interest to traders in general. If we don't carry it in stock, we can generally quote you a price and have the book shipped to you direct from the publisher. Please write us at the above address, and we will gladly forward you our current "Trader's Catalog" by return mail.

EDWARD DOBSON
GREENVILLE, S.C.

TRADER'S PRESS, INC.
P.O. BOX 10344
GREENVILLE, S.C. 29603

BOOKS FOR STOCK
AND COMMODITY
TRADERS

NOTICE OF FREE RECOMMENDATION SERVICE

There are literally hundreds of books available on the many
aspects of stock and commodity trading. Many of these books are quite
expensive, with the price of some exceeding $100. We have spent years
dealing with books in this field, and feel we have a good idea of which
of the many books available represent the best quality material and would
give you the best value for your money. If you are interested in building
a reference library of books on trading, and you would like our opinion
on the best books available on a given topic area, for example, technical
analysis, charting, trading systems, etc., please write us a note at the
address above with your daytime and evening phones, the best time to call,
and the topics you wish to cover; we will either send you a written list-
ing of our recommendations or give you a return call to discuss same. Be
aware that our primary area of specialty is commodities, with an emphasis
on technical analysis and trading methods and systems.

EDWARD DOBSON
GREENVILLE, S.C.

TRADER'S PRESS, INC.
P.O. BOX 10344
GREENVILLE, S.C. 29603

BOOKS FOR STOCK
AND COMMODITY
TRADERS

Publishers of:

Commodity Spreads: A Historical Chart Perspective (Dobson)
Commodity Spreads: Volume 2 (Dobson)
The Trading Rule That Can Make You Rich * (Dobson)
Viewpoints of A Commodity Trader (Longstreet)
Commodities: A Chart Anthology (Dobson)
Profitable Grain Trading (Ainsworth)
A Complete Guide to Trading Profits (Paris)
Trader's Guide To Technical Analysis (Hardy)
The Professional Commodity Trader (Kroll)
Jesse Livermore: Speculator-King (Sarnoff)
Reminiscences of a Stock Operator (Lefevre)
Understanding Fibonacci Numbers (Dobson)

Please write for our current catalog describing these and many other books
of interest to traders.